A SIMPLE SERIES EASTER

PRESENTS

WORTHY IS THE LAMB

A 24-MINUTE MINI-MUSICAL ARRANGED ESPECIALLY FOR UNISON AND TWO-PART CHOIRS

Created by Sue C. Smith and Mason Brown

AVAILABLE PRODUCTS:

Choral Book	45757-2618-7
CD Preview Pak	45757-2618-1
Listening CD	45757-2618-2
Split-Track Accompaniment CD	45757-2618-3
Split-Track Accompaniment DVD	45757-2618-6
Soprano/Alto Rehearsal Track CD	45757-2618-0
Tenor/Bass Rehearsal Track CD	45757-2618-5

www.brentwoodbenson.com

a division of

BRENTWOOD
MUSIC
PUBLICATIONS

BRENTWOOD-BENSON
music publications

© MMXIV Brentwood-Benson Music Publications,
101 Winners Circle, Brentwood, TN 37027.

Contents

Glorious, Glorious

Words and Music by
JOEL LINDSEY
and **JEFF BUMGARDNER**
Arranged by Daniel Semsen

Glo-ri-ous, glo-ri-ous, let us_ re-joice.

Glo-ri-ous, glo-ri-ous, lift-ing our voice. We who were hope-less

Lord, You are glo - ri - ous! Glo - ri - ous, glo - ri - ous,

let us__ re - joice. Glo - ri - ous, glo - ri - ous, lift - ing our voice.

We who were hope-less are now vic-to-ri-ous. Praise our Re-deem-er.

Glo - ri - ous, glo - ri - ous,_____ glo - ri - ous, glo - ri -

NARRATOR: Blessed be the God and Father of our Lord Jesus Christ, who according to His great mercy has caused us to be born again to a living hope through the resurrection of Jesus Christ from the dead, to *obtain* an inheritance *which is* imperishable and undefiled and will not fade away, reserved in heaven for you, … *(I Peter 1:3-4 NASB)*

Glo - ri - ous, glo - ri - ous, let us__ re - joice.

Glo - ri - ous, glo - ri - ous, lift - ing__ our voice.

Hail Jesus Medley

Victory Chant / Because We Believe

Arranged by Russell Mauldin

NARRATOR: *(Music starts)* Jesus had come to earth on a mission ordained from the world's beginning. He had emptied Himself of His glory and lived as a servant. He had healed the sick, embraced the outcast, and taught all who would listen. Now the time had come to lay down His life. *(Music changes)* It was the beginning of Passover, and as word of His arrival in Jerusalem spread, a spontaneous celebration began.

55

How pow - er - ful You are.____

How pow - er - ful You are.

Am/G G Am/G G

57

Hail, hail, Li - on of Ju - dah.____

Hail, hail, Li - on of Ju - dah.

G Am/G G Am/G G Am/G G Am/G G

59 17

How won - der - ful You are.____

How won - der - ful You are.

Am/G G Am/G G

BECAUSE WE BELIEVE (Jamie Harvill, Nancy Gordon)

In Christ Alone

Words and Music by
KEITH GETTY and STUART TOWNEND
Arranged by Bradley Knight

NARRATOR: His last week was filled with confrontation with those who would destroy Him, tenderness for those who would grieve for Him, compassion for those who would fail Him, *(Music starts)* and sorrow for even the one who would betray Him. Jesus knew how He would die, and He understood why He must. He showed us with every word, every gesture, every interaction, what it would take to save us, for He alone was worthy to interpose His blood between our sin and God's wrath.

26

cross   as Je-sus died,   the wrath of God   was sat-is-
fied.   For ev-'ry sin   on Him was laid,___   here in the
death of Christ   I   live.

31

home, here in the pow'r of Christ I'll stand. No pow'r of

hell, no scheme of man, can ev - er pluck me from His

Drums cont.

hand. Till He re - turns or calls me home,___ here in the

rit.

pow'r of Christ I'll stand.

rit.

Jesus Paid It All

Words and Music by
ELVINA M. HALL and JOHN T. GRAPE
Arranged by Travis Cottrell and David Moffitt

NARRATOR: *(Music starts)* Let's sing this together as we worship.

washed it white as snow.

Sin had left a crim-son stain.

He washed it white as snow.

Agnus Dei
with Worthy Is the Lamb

Words and Music by
MICHAEL W. SMITH
Arranged by Richard Kingsmore

NARRATOR: With the words "It is finished," Jesus took His last breath. After His death, a rich man named Joseph found the courage to ask Pilate for the Lord's body. It seemed as if His story had come to a tragic end. But Heaven had another plan. On Sunday, tragedy was replaced by victory. *(Music starts)* Sorrow turned into celebration. Lament gave way to hallelujahs. And the song of praise that began at the empty tomb is still our song today.

36

Je - sus, Son of God,___ the dar - ling of heav - en cru-

- ci - fied.___

Wor - thy is__ the Lamb,__ seat - ed on__ the throne.

Crown You now with man - y crowns, You

That's Why We Praise Him
with Alleluia! Alleluia!

Words and Music by
TOMMY WALKER
Arranged by Russell Mauldin

NARRATOR: *(Music starts)* Our worship is filled with songs that declare our unworthiness and His holiness, our need and His compassion, our hopelessness and His salvation. This is why we sing, why we bow, why we surrender our lives. For Jesus alone is worthy and we will worship Him forever. *(Music changes)* While we live on this earth, until He returns, we'll tell His story and declare our devotion and love for Him to the world.

That's why we bow __ down and wor-ship this King, 'cause He

gave His ev - 'ry-thing. He gave His ev - 'ry-

thing. ___

ALLELUIA! ALLELUIA! (Christopher Wordsworth, Ludwig van Beethoven)